THE
TESTING-TREE

Also by STANLEY KUNITZ

INTELLECTUAL THINGS

PASSPORT TO THE WAR

SELECTED POEMS 1928–1958

THE
TESTING-TREE

Poems by
Stanley Kunitz

An Atlantic Monthly Press Book
LITTLE, BROWN AND COMPANY · BOSTON · TORONTO

LIBRARY OF CONGRESS CATALOG CARD NO. 75-143704

FIRST EDITION

ATLANTIC—LITTLE, BROWN BOOKS
ARE PUBLISHED BY
LITTLE, BROWN AND COMPANY
IN ASSOCIATION WITH
THE ATLANTIC MONTHLY PRESS

Published simultaneously in Canada
by Little, Brown & Company (Canada) Limited

PRINTED IN THE UNITED STATES OF AMERICA

For Elise

Author's Note

Some of the poems in this volume have previously appeared in the *Atlantic, Art in America, Book Week, New American Review, The New Leader, The New York Quarterly, The New York Review of Books, The New York Times, Partisan Review, Poetry, The Times Literary Supplement* (London). The poem "The Magic Curtain" appeared originally in *The New Yorker*.

Contents

I

JOURNAL FOR MY DAUGHTER

1

Your turn. Grass of confusion.
You say you had a father once:
his name was absence.
He left, but did not let you go.
Part of him, more than a shadow,
beckoned down corridors,
secret, elusive, saturnine,
melting at your touch.
In the crack
of a divided house
grew the resentment-weed.
It has white inconspicuous flowers.
Family of anthologists!
Collectors of injuries!

2

I wake to a glittering world,
to the annunciation of the frost.
A popeyed chipmunk scurries past,
the pockets of his cheeks bulging.
As the field mice store seeds,
as the needle-nosed shrew
threading under the woodpile
deposits little heaps of land-snails
for milestones on its runways,
I propose

that we gather our affections.
Lambkin, I care.

3

I was happy you were born,
your banks of digits
equipped for decimals,
and all your clever parts
neatly in place.
Your nation gives me joy,
as it has always given.
If I could have my choice
on the way to exile
I think I'd rather sleep forever
than wake up cold
in a country without women.

4

You cried. You cried.
You wasted and you cried.
Night after night
I walked the floor with you,
croaking the same old
tranquillizing song,
the only tune
I ever learned to carry.
In the rosy tissue
of your brain,
where memory begins,
that theme is surely scored,
waiting till you need
to play it back.
There were three crows
sat on a tree

Sing Billy Magee Magaw.
You do not need to sing to me.
I like the sound of your voice
even when you phone from school
asking for money.

5

There was a big blond uncle-bear,
wounded, smoke-eyed, wild,
who shambled from the west
with his bags full of havoc.
He spoke the bears' grunt-language,
waving his paws
and rocking on his legs.
Both of us were drunk,
slapping each other on the back,
sweaty with genius.
He spouted his nonsense-rhymes,
roaring like a behemoth.
You crawled under the sofa.

6

Goodies are shaken
from the papa-tree:
*Be what you are. Give
what is yours to give.
Have style. Dare.*
Such a storm of fortune cookies!
Outside your room
stands the white-headed prowler
in his multiple disguises
who reminds you of your likeness.
Wherever you turn,
down whatever street,

in the fugues of appetite,
in the groin of nightmare,
he waits for you,
haggard with his thousand years.
His agents are everywhere,
his heart is at home
in your own generation;
the folded message in his hands
is stiff with dirt and wine-stains,
older than the Dead Sea Scrolls.
Daughter, read:
What do I want of my life?
More! More!

7

Demonstrations in the streets.
I am there not there,
ever uneasy in a crowd.
But you belong,
flaunting your home-made
insubordinate flag.
Why should I be surprised?
We come of a flinty maverick line.
In my father's time, I'm told,
our table was set in turn
for Maxim Gorky, Emma Goldman,
and the atheist Ingersoll.
If your slogan is mis-spelt
Don't tred on me!
still it strikes
parents and politicians down.
Noli me tangere! is what
I used to cry in Latin once.
Oh to be radical, young, desirable, cool!

8

Your first dog was a Pekinese,
fat and saucy Ko-San,
half mandarin, half mini-lion,
who chased milkmen and mailmen
and bit the tires of every passing car
till a U.S. Royal bit him back.
You sobbed for half an hour,
then romped to the burial service
in the lower garden
by the ferny creek.
I helped you pick the stones
to mark his shallow grave.
It was the summer I went away.
One night I carried you outdoors,
in a blitz of fireflies,
to watch your first eclipse.
Your far-off voice,
drugged with milk and sleep,
said it was a leaf
sliding over the light.

9

The night when Coleridge,
heavy-hearted,
bore his crying child outside,
he noted
that those brimming eyes
caught the reflection
of the starry sky,
and each suspended tear
made a sparkling moon.

THE ILLUMINATION

In that hotel my life
rolled in its socket
twisting my strings.
All my mistakes,
from my earliest
bedtimes,
rose against me:
the parent I denied,
the friends I failed,
the hearts I spoiled,
including at least
my own left ventricle —
a history of shame.
"Dante!" I cried
to the apparition
entering from the hall,
laureled and gaunt,
in a cone of light.

"Out of mercy you came
to be my Master
and my guide!"
To which he replied:
"I know neither the time
nor the way
nor the number on the door . . .
but this must be my room,
I was here before."
And he held up in his hand
the key,
which blinded me.

THREE FLOORS

Mother was a crack of light
and a gray eye peeping;
I made believe by breathing hard
that I was sleeping.

Sister's doughboy on last leave
had robbed me of her hand;
downstairs at intervals she played
Warum on the baby grand.

Under the roof a wardrobe trunk
whose lock a boy could pick
contained a red Masonic hat
and a walking stick.

Bolt upright in my bed that night
I saw my father flying;
the wind was walking on my neck,
the windowpanes were crying.

THE FLIGHT OF APOLLO

1

Earth was my home, but even there I was a
stranger. This mineral crust. I walk like a
swimmer. What titanic bombardments in
those old astral wars! I know what I know: I
shall never escape from strangeness or com-
plete my journey. Think of me as nostalgic,
afraid, exalted. I am your man on the moon,
a speck of megalomania, restless for the
leap toward island universes pulsing beyond
where the constellations set. Infinite space
overwhelms the human heart, but in the middle of nowhere life inexorably calls to life.
Forward my mail to Mars. What news from
the Great Spiral Nebula in Andromeda and
the Magellanic Clouds?

2

I was a stranger on earth.
Stepping on the moon, I begin
the gay pilgrimage to new
Jerusalems
in foreign galaxies.
Heat. Cold. Craters of silence.
The Sea of Tranquillity
rolling on the shores of entropy.
And, beyond,
the intelligence of the stars.

AROUND PASTOR BONHOEFFER

THE PLOT AGAINST HITLER

Jittery, missing their cues,
Bach's glory jailed in their throats,
they were clustered round the piano
in the Biedermeier parlor,
sisters and brothers
and their brothers by marriage,
rehearsing a cantata
for Papa's seventy-fifth birthday.
Kyrie eleison: Night
like no other night, plotted
and palmed,
omega of terror,
packed like a bullet
in the triggered chamber.
Surely the men had arrived at their stations.
Through the staves of the music
he saw their target strutting,
baring its malignant heart.
Lord, let the phone ring!
Let the phone ring!

NEXT TO LAST THINGS

Slime, in the grains of the State,
like smut in the corn,
from the top infected.
Hatred made law,

wolves bred out of maggots
rolling in blood,
and the seal of the church ravished
to receive the crooked sign.
All the steeples were burning.
In the chapel of his ear
he had heard the midnight bells
jangling: *if you permit*
this evil, what is the good
of the good of your life?
And he forsook the last things,
the dear inviolable mysteries —
Plato's lamp, passed from the hand
of saint to saint —
that he might risk his soul in the streets,
where the things given
are only next to last;
in God's name cheating, pretending,
playing the double agent,
choosing to trade
the prayer for the deed,
and the deed most vile.
I am a liar and a traitor.

THE EXTERMINATION CAMP

Through the half-open door of the hut
the camp doctor saw him kneeling,
with his hands quietly folded.
"I was most deeply moved by the way
this lovable man prayed,
so devout and so certain
that God heard his prayer."
Round-faced, bespectacled, mild,

candid with costly grace,
he walked toward the gallows
and did not falter.
Oh but he knew the Hangman!
Only a few steps more
and he would enter the arcanum
where the Master
would take him by the shoulder,
as He does at each encounter,
and turn him round
to face his brothers in the world.

KING OF THE RIVER

If the water were clear enough,
if the water were still,
but the water is not clear,
the water is not still,
you would see yourself,
slipped out of your skin,
nosing upstream,
slapping, thrashing,
tumbling
over the rocks
till you paint them
with your belly's blood:
Finned Ego,
yard of muscle that coils,
uncoils.

If the knowledge were given you,
but it is not given,
for the membrane is clouded
with self-deceptions
and the iridescent image swims
through a mirror that flows,
you would surprise yourself
in that other flesh
heavy with milt,
bruised, battering towards the dam
that lips the orgiastic pool.

Come. Bathe in these waters.
Increase and die.

If the power were granted you
to break out of your cells,
but the imagination fails
and the doors of the senses close
on the child within,
you would dare to be changed,
as you are changing now,
into the shape you dread
beyond the merely human.
A dry fire eats you.
Fat drips from your bones.
The flutes of your gills discolor.
You have become a ship for parasites.
The great clock of your life
is slowing down,
and the small clocks run wild.
For this you were born.
You have cried to the wind
and heard the wind's reply:
"I did not choose the way,
the way chose me."
You have tasted the fire on your tongue
till it is swollen black
with a prophetic joy:
"Burn with me!
The only music is time,
the only dance is love."

If the heart were pure enough,
but it is not pure,
you would admit

that nothing compels you
any more, nothing
at all abides,
but nostalgia and desire,
the two-way ladder
between heaven and hell.
On the threshold
of the last mystery,
at the brute absolute hour,
you have looked into the eyes
of your creature self,
which are glazed with madness,
and you say
he is not broken but endures,
limber and firm
in the state of his shining,
forever inheriting his salt kingdom,
from which he is banished
forever.

II

THE MULCH

A man with a leaf in his head
watches an indefatigable gull
dropping a piss-clam on the rocks
to break it open.
Repeat. Repeat.
He is an inlander
who loves the margins of the sea,
and everywhere he goes he carries
a bag of earth on his back.
Why is he down in the tide marsh?
Why is he gathering salt hay
in bushel baskets crammed to his chin?
"It is a blue and northern air,"
he says, as if the shiftings of the sky
had taught him husbandry.
Birthdays for him are when he wakes
and falls into the news of weather.
"Try! Try!" clicks the beetle in his wrist,
his heart is an educated swamp,
and he is mindful of his garden,
which prepares to die.

ROBIN REDBREAST

It was the dingiest bird
you ever saw, all the color
washed from him, as if
he had been standing in the rain,
friendless and stiff and cold,
since Eden went wrong.
In the house marked For Sale,
where nobody made a sound,
in the room where I lived
with an empty page, I had heard
the squawking of the jays
under the wild persimmons
tormenting him.
So I scooped him up
after they knocked him down,
in league with that ounce of heart
pounding in my palm,
that dumb beak gaping.
Poor thing! Poor foolish life!
without sense enough to stop
running in desperate circles,
needing my lucky help
to toss him back into his element.
But when I held him high,
fear clutched my hand,
for through the hole in his head,
cut whistle-clean . . .
through the old dried wound

between his eyes
where the hunter's brand
had tunneled out his wits . . .
I caught the cold flash of the blue
unappeasable sky.

INDIAN SUMMER AT LAND'S END

The season stalls, unseasonably fair,
blue-fair, serene, a stack of golden discs,
each disc a day, and the addition slow.
I wish you were here with me to walk the flats,
towards dusk especially when the tide is out
and the bay turns opal, filled with rolling fire
that washes on the mouldering wreck offshore,
our mussel-vineyard, strung with bearded grapes.
Last night I reached for you and shaped you there
lying beside me as we drifted past
the farthest seamarks and the watchdog bells,
and round Long Point throbbing its frosty light,
until we streamed into the open sea.
What did I know of voyaging till now?
Meanwhile I tend my flock, strange golden puffs
diminutive as wrens, with snipped-off tails,
who bounce down from the trees. High overhead,
on the trackless roads, skywriting V and yet
another V, the southbound Canada express
hoots of horizons and distances . . . .

SUMMER SOLSTICE

— from Osip Mandelstam

Orioles live in the elms, and in classical verse
the length of the vowels alone determines the measure.
Once and once only a year nature knows quantity
stretched to the limit, as in Homer's meter.

O this is a day that yawns like a caesura:
serene from the start, almost painfully slowed.
Oxen browse in the field, and a golden languor
keeps me from drawing a rich, whole note from my reed.

TRISTIA

— from Osip Mandelstam

I made myself an expert in farewells
by studying laments, the nightfall of a woman's hair.
Oxen chew their cud; anticipation lags;
it is the town's last restless hour;
and I praise that ritual night when the cocks crowed
and eyelids, heavy with the griefs that pass,
opened to the light, while her weeping flowed
into the sound of the Muses singing.

Who knows, when the time comes to say goodbye,
what separation we are meant to bear
and what for us cockcrow shall signify
when the acropolis burns like a flare,
and why, at the new daybreak of a life,
when the ox is ruminating in his stall,
the herald cock, prophetic of rebirth,
should flap his wings on the town wall?

I bless the craft of spinning: the to-and-fro
action of the shuttle, the way the spindle hums.
Look! barefooted Delia, light as a feather,
hurries to meet you, flying as she comes.
Oh, how scrawny is the language of joy,
that weak foundation of our mortal lot!
Everything happened before; it will happen again.
Only the flash of recognition brings delight.

Be it so: a small transparent puppet lies,
like a dried squirrel-skin
extended on a plate,
while a girl crouches, staring, over the image.
Wax is for women what bronze is for men.
We, who move blindly toward a world of shades,
only in battle dare confront our fate, —
but their gift is to die while telling fortunes.

AFTER THE LAST DYNASTY

Reading in Li Po
how "the peach blossom follows the water"
I keep thinking of you
because you were so much like
Chairman Mao,
naturally with the sex
transposed
and the figure slighter.
Loving you was a kind
of Chinese guerrilla war.
Thanks to your lightfoot genius
no Eighth Route Army
kept its lines more fluid,
traveled with less baggage,
so nibbled the advantage.
Even with your small bad heart
you made a dance of departures.
In the cold spring rains
when last you failed me
I had nothing left to spend
but a red crayon language
on the character of the enemy
to break appointments,
to fight us not
with his strength
but with his weakness,
to kill us

not with his health
but with his sickness.

Pet, spitfire, blue-eyed pony,
here is a new note
I want to pin on your door,
though I am ten years late
and you are nowhere:
Tell me,
are you still mistress of the valley,
what trophies drift downriver,
why did you keep me waiting?

RIVER ROAD

That year of the cloud, when my marriage failed,
I slept in a chair, by the flagstone hearth,
fighting my sleep,
and one night saw a Hessian soldier
stand at attention there in full
regalia, till his head broke into flames.
My only other callers were the FBI
sent to investigate me as a Russian spy
by patriotic neighbors on the river road;
and flying squirrels parachuting from the elms
who squeaked in rodent heat between the walls
and upstairs rumbled at their nutty games.
I never dared open the attic door.
Even my nervous Leghorns joined the act,
indulging their taste for chicken from behind.
A glazed look swam into the survivors' eyes;
they caught a sort of dancing-sickness,
a variation of the blind staggers,
that hunched their narrow backs, and struck
a stiffened wing akimbo,
as round and round the poultry yard
they flapped and dropped and flapped again.
The county agent shook his head:
not one of them was spared the cyanide.

That year of the cloud, when my marriage failed,
I paced up and down the bottom-fields,
tamping the mud-puddled nurslings in

with a sharp blow of the heel
timed to the chop-chop of the hoe:
red pine and white, larch, balsam fir,
one stride apart, two hundred to the row,
until I heard from Rossiter's woods
the downward spiral of a veery's song
unwinding on the eve of war.

Lord! Lord! who has lived so long?
Count it ten thousand trees ago,
five houses and ten thousand trees,
since the swallows exploded from Bowman Tower
over the place where the hermit sang,
while I held a fantail of squirming roots
that kissed the palm of my dirty hand,
as if in reply to a bird.
The stranger who hammers No Trespass signs
to the staghorn sumac along the road
must think he owns this property.
I park my car below the curve
and climbing over the tumbled stones
where the wild foxgrape perseveres,
I walk into the woods I made,
my dark and resinous, blistered land,
through the deep litter of the years.

THE MAGIC CURTAIN

1

At breakfast mother sipped her buttermilk,
    her mind already on her shop,
    unrolling gingham by the yard,
stitching her dresses for the Boston trade.
Behind her, Frieda with the yellow hair,
    capricious keeper of the toast,
    buckled her knees, as if she'd lost
balance and platter, then winked at me, blue-eyed.
Frieda, my first love! who sledded me to sleep
    through snows of the Bavarian woods
    into the bell-song of the girls,
with kinds of kisses mother would not dream;
tales of her wicked stepfather, a dwarf,
    from whom she fled to Bremerhaven
    with scarcely the tatters on her back;
riddles, nonsense, lieder, counting-songs. . . .
        Ein, zwei, drei, vier, fünf, sechs, sieben,
        Wo ist hier mein liebster Herr geblieben?
        Er ist nicht hier, er ist nicht da,
        Er is fort nach Amerika.
"Be sure," said mother briskly at the door,
    "that you get Sonny off to school
    on time. And see that he combs his hair."
How could she guess what we two had in mind?

2

Downtown at the Front St. Bi-jo (spelt Bijou)
    we were, as always, the first in line,
    with a hot nickel clutched in hand,

impatient for *The Perils of Pauline*,
my Frieda in her dainty blouse and skirt,
    I in my starched white sailor suit
    and buttoned shoes, prepared to hang
from cliffs, twist on a rack, be tied to rails.
School faded out at every morning reel,
    The Iron Claw held me in thrall,
    Cabiria taught me the Punic Wars,
at bloody Antietam I fought on Griffith's side.
And Keystone Kops came tumbling on the scene
    in outsized uniforms, moustached,
    their thick-browed faces dipped in flour,
to crank tin lizzies that immediately collapsed.
John Bunny held his belly when he laughed,
    ladies politely removed their hats,
    Cyrus of Persia stormed the gates,
upsetting our orgy at Belshazzar's Feast.
Then Charlie shuffled in on bunioned feet.
    We twirled with him an imaginary cane
    and blew our noses for the gallant poor
who bet on a horse, the horse that always loses.
Blanche Sweet, said Frieda, had a pretty name,
    but I came back with Arline Pretty,
    and, even sweeter, Louise Lovely.
Send me your picture, Violet Mersereau!
Lights up! Ushers with atomizers ranged
    the aisles, emitting lilac spray.
    We lunched on peanuts and Hershey bars
and moved to the Majestic for the two o'clock show.

3

Five . . . four . . . three . . . two . . . one . . .
    The frames are whirling backward, see!
    The operator's lost control.

Your story flickers on your bedroom wall.
Deaths, marriages, betrayals, lies,
  close-ups of tears, forbidden games,
  spill in a montage on a screen,
with chases, pratfalls, custard pies, and sores.
You have become your past, which time replays,
  to your surprise, as comedy.
  That coathanger neatly whisked your coat
right off your back. Soon it will want your skin.
  Five . . four . . three . . two . . one . .
  Where has my dearest gone?
  She is nowhere to be found,
  She dwells in the underground.
Let the script revel in tricks and transformations.
  When the film is broken, let it be spliced
  where Frieda vanished one summer night
with somebody's husband, daddy to a brood.
And with her vanished, from the bureau drawer,
  the precious rose-enameled box
  that held those chestnut-colored curls
clipped from my sorrowing head when I was four.
After the war an unsigned picture-card
  from Dresden came, with one word: *Liebe.*
  "I'll never forgive her," mother said,
but as for me, I do and do and do.

III

THE SYSTEM

That pack of scoundrels
tumbling through the gate
emerges
as the Order of the State.

HAND-ROLLED CIGARETTES

— from Yevgeny Yevtushenko

If, in a fisherman's hut, you poke
behind the sagging sideboard with a stick,
you'll find his stock for making cigarettes,
a pile of newspapers, many-years-thick.

There you'll meet mobs of secret agents
and doctor-poisoners of the age.
Bedbugs and roaches with moustaches
huddle, and crawl along the page.

Returning late, the tired fisherman
enjoys his ladled kvass's tang,
and sifts tobacco at his ease
onto some bureaucrat's harangue.

Cool in the practice of his skill,
with fingers confident and strong,
he coils the speech in a narrow tube
and neatly wets it with his tongue.

The contents? — they're not his affair!
That glowing edge of nicotine
advancing, at the end of day,
eats up the newsprint, line by line.

He would have liked a sunny day,
wind in his sails and a lucky catch.
His yellow nail gleams salmon-bright,
flicking dead words reduced to ash.

Old eulogies and exposés
fulfill their destiny and rise,
with trashy articles and poems,
in spiral columns to the skies.

When evening falls in the north country,
cigarette-tips pinpoint the gray,
as, caught in the mood of dirty weather,
fishermen sit and puff away.

Their worn tobacco pouches rustle
till dawn sweeps inland on the tide.
Listen! they roll another cigarette:
and history is on their side.

THE CUSTOMS COLLECTOR'S REPORT

For the sake of the record:
  on Tuesday, the 19th instant,
the third day of the storm,
  shortly before nightfall,
they swam over the pass together,
  this pair in their battered armor,
first seen in my spyglass;
  stovepipes assisting each other,
cylinders skating the snowcrust,
  comedians sprawling,
now and then dropping
  under the surface,
perceptible only
  as mounds in the driftage.

To whom, in this trial,
  could I turn for instructions?

At the north wall of the gorge,
  where zero poured to its funnel,
in the absence of guidelines
  I dared the encounter,
half-digging them out
  from the coils of the blizzard,
half-dying of cold
  as I scratched at the ice pack.
Then came issue of smothered voices,
  wind rumbling in empty barrels,

the sound of flags flapping
 in a cave of the mountain;
and the words that I heard
 flew by in tatters:
"nothing . . . nothing to declare . . .
 our wounds speak . . . heroes . . .
unfairly ambushed . . . the odds impossible . . .
 let our countrymen know . . . pride . . .
  honor . . .
how bravely . . . and oh
 what a body-count! . . ."
And the thinner voice cried,
 plaintively winding,
"True, brother, true! but tell me —
 what was the name of our war?"
When I lifted their helmets
 a gas escaped from them,
putrid, as from all battlefields,
 the last breath of the human.
That moment they were lightened.
 It seemed the earth shuddered,
the white tombs opened,
 disgorging their breastplates.
I saw them rise in the wind
 and roll off like ashcans.

Dear sirs, my lords, this
 is a lonely post,
what can I ask but your compassion?
 I petition you for transfer.

THE GLADIATORS

They fought in heavy armor
or, nimbly, with net and trident;
if lucky, against wild beasts,
but mostly against their brothers.

Criminals, captives, slaves,
what did they have to lose?
And the cheers egged them on,
as they waded through shit and blood.

When Claudius gave the sign
the throats of the fallen were cut
in the shade of the royal box:
he fancied their dying looks.

Domitian's coarser itch
was to set cripples on cripples.
No entertainment matched
the sport of their hacking and bleating.

Trajan's phantasmagoric show,
lasting a hundred days,
used up five thousand pairs
of jocks — and the count resumes.

A monk climbs out of the stands,
he is running onto the field,
he is waving his scrawny arms
to interrupt the games.

The mob tears him to bits.
Tomorrow the gates will be closed,
but the promised Crusades will start
with a torchlight children's parade.

BOLSHEVIKS

— from Aba Stolzenberg

They came on ponies, barefoot,
brandishing guns that had no bullets;
wore ladies' hats backwards; their leaders
with the look of deacons; and packs
of ox-men, heads wrapped in sacks.

They came in early autumn, shook down
the pears they could not pick by hand;
sprawled across sidewalks and church steps
and felt themselves masters of the land.

The motorcycles spring out of nowhere.
A blast from the roaring White Guards!
Of Trotsky's soldiers nothing remains here
but some sad little mounds near the woods.

44

THE MOUND BUILDERS

"Macon is the seventh layer of civilization on this spot."
— *inscription at Ocmulgee National Monument, Georgia*

1

Let the old geezers jig on Penn-
sylvania Avenue, and when the jig ends
let them offer a cracked tune
in praise of power:
the State counts the teeth of its friends.
All month, knee-deep in South,
oiled by Methodist money,
I have whirled to a different music
with oversweet, underdeveloped girls
who make me missionary.
My daughter sits in every class;
love is the tongue in my mouth.
Today through the streets of the Greek Revival
and the confederacy of the lawns
trumpeting with azaleas,
my rented Falcon flies
from the tiresome sound of my own voice,
the courteous chicken sitting on my plate,
and Sidney Lanier's exhausted flute
stuck in its cabinet of glass.
What's best in me lives underground,
rooting and digging, itching for wings;
my very worst imaginings
I give to the spoilers of the air.
At the National Park under a sky

of unshattered, unshatterable blue
I rejoice in the prevalence of green
and the starry chickweed of the fields;
through the millennial ordeal
part, if only part of me, goes down
to the master farmers who built this mound,
this ceremonial earth-lodge,
and locked an eagle in it, shaped of clay,
the fork-eyed spotted bird of their cult,
and piled their dead in mounds higher and higher,
and raised up temple-mounds
to the giver of breath and corn
on which they stacked the harvest fire
that lit this stage for two hundred years.
Fifteen square miles! They must have known their power
stopped by the willows at the river's edge,
and yet it was too much to hold:
only their ghost-song haunts the field.

2

Musician of the lost tribes,
you summon to the council chamber,
to the elders in their scooped-out circle,
an earth-faced chorus of the lost,
people without name to remember,
led by stallion-proud Emperor Brim
bearing his feathered calumet,
chief of the tall Cowetas,
father of the Creek Nation,
by the Spaniards called "Gran Cazique,"
most feared redman of his generation;
forshadowed, as a scroll unwinds,
by potters out of the swamps
who set their mark on the fanciful pipes they smoked

in the figure of birds or humans,
makers of bowls with carinated shoulders;
and their distant cousins, a patient cloud,
upholding jars with a smooth fold of the lip;
and, more dimly still, the shellfish eaters,
people of the stone axe,
who pitched their noisome camps
on their garbage heaps;
and straggling far behind,
out of primeval murk,
those wandering hunters in search of food
who crossed the land-bridge of the Bering Strait
and sliding over the glacier's edge
paved our first trails with their Mongol bones.
They followed the game that they pursued
into museums of prehistory,
featureless but for the fluted points
dropped from the bloodied mammoth's flanks.

3

The mounds rise up on every side
of a seven-layered world, as I stand
in the middle of the Ocmulgee fields,
by the Central of Georgia Railway track,
with the Creek braves under my feet
and the City of Macon at my back.

IV

BORIS PASTERNAK

— from Anna Akhmatova

He who has compared himself with the eye of a horse
peers, looks, sees, identifies,
and instantly like molten diamonds
puddles shine, ice grieves and liquefies.

In lilac mists the backyards drowse,
and depots, logs, leaves, clouds above;
that hooting train, that crunch of watermelon rind,
that timid hand in a perfumed kid glove . . .

All's ringing, roaring, grinding, breakers' crash —
and silence all at once, release;
it means he is tiptoeing over pine needles,
so as not to startle the light sleep of space.

And it means he is counting the grains
in the blasted ears; it means
he has come again to the Daryal Wall,
accursed and black, from another funeral.

And again Moscow, where the heart's fever burns;
far off the deadly sleighbell chimes;
someone is lost two steps from home
in waist-high snow. The worst of times . . .

For having compared smoke with the Laocoön,
for making a song out of graveyard thistles,
for filling the world with a new sound
of verse reverberating in new space,

he has been rewarded by a kind of eternal childhood,
with the generosity and brilliance of the stars;
the whole of the earth was his to inherit,
and his to share with every human spirit.

DANTE

. . . mio bel San Giovanni

— from Anna Akhmatova

Even after his death he did not return
to the city that nursed him.
Going away, this man did not look back.
To him I sing this song.
Torches, night, a last embrace,
outside in her streets the mob howling.
He sent her a curse from hell
and in heaven could not forget her.
But never, in a penitent's shirt,
did he walk barefoot with lighted candle
through his beloved Florence,
perfidious, base, and irremediably home.

CLEOPATRA

— from Anna Akhmatova

She had already kissed Antony's dead lips,
she had already wept on her knees before Caesar . . .
and her servants have betrayed her. Darkness falls.
The trumpets of the Roman eagle scream.

And in comes the last man to be ravished by her
      beauty —
such a tall gallant! — with a shamefaced whisper:
"You must walk before him, as a slave, in the triumph."
But the slope of her swan's neck is tranquil as ever.

Tomorrow they'll put her children in chains. Nothing
remains except to tease this fellow out of mind
and put the black snake, like a parting act of pity,
on her dark breast with indifferent hand.

THE ARTIST

His paintings grew darker every year.
They filled the walls, they filled the room;
eventually they filled his world —
all but the ravishment.
When voices faded, he would rush to hear
the scratched soul of Mozart
endlessly in gyre.
Back and forth, back and forth,
he paced the paint-smeared floor,
diminishing in size each time he turned,
trapped in his monumental void,
raving against his adversaries.
At last he took a knife in his hand
and slashed an exit for himself
between the frames of his tall scenery.
Through the holes of his tattered universe
the first innocence and the light
came pouring in.

THE BOTTOM OF THE GLASS

Not by planning and not by choosing
I learned the mastery.
What a damnable trade
where winning is like losing!
The wheel keeps spinning,
the thread gets broken,
my hand cannot tell
its work from its loafing.
Life aims at the tragic:
what makes it ridiculous?
In age as in youth
the joke is preposterous.
And nothing shall save me
from meanness and sinning
but more of the same,
more losing like winning.

THE PORTRAIT

My mother never forgave my father
for killing himself,
especially at such an awkward time
and in a public park,
that spring
when I was waiting to be born.
She locked his name
in her deepest cabinet
and would not let him out,
though I could hear him thumping.
When I came down from the attic
with the pastel portrait in my hand
of a long-lipped stranger
with a brave moustache
and deep brown level eyes,
she ripped it into shreds
without a single word
and slapped me hard.
In my sixty-fourth year
I can feel my cheek
still burning.

AN OLD CRACKED TUNE

My name is Solomon Levi,
the desert is my home,
my mother's breast was thorny,
and father I had none.

The sands whispered, *Be separate*,
the stones taught me, *Be hard.*
I dance, for the joy of surviving,
on the edge of the road.

AGAIN! AGAIN!

Love knocked again at my door:
I tossed her a bucket of bones.
From each bone springs a soldier
who shoots me as a stranger.

THE TESTING-TREE

1

On my way home from school
    up tribal Providence Hill
        past the Academy ballpark
where I could never hope to play
    I scuffed in the drainage ditch
        among the sodden seethe of leaves
hunting for perfect stones
    rolled out of glacial time
        into my pitcher's hand;
then sprinted lickety-
    split on my magic Keds
        from a crouching start,
scarcely touching the ground
    with my flying skin
        as I poured it on
for the prize of the mastery
    over that stretch of road,
        with no one no where to deny
when I flung myself down
    that on the given course
        I was the world's fastest human.

2

Around the bend
    that tried to loop me home
        dawdling came natural

across a nettled field
    riddled with rabbit-life
        where the bees sank sugar-wells
in the trunks of the maples
    and a stringy old lilac
        more than two stories tall
blazing with mildew
    remembered a door in the
        long teeth of the woods.
All of it happened slow:
    brushing the stickseed off,
        wading through jewelweed
strangled by angel's hair,
    spotting the print of the deer
        and the red fox's scats.

Once I owned the key
    to an umbrageous trail
        thickened with mosses
where flickering presences
    gave me right of passage
        as I followed in the steps
of straight-backed Massassoit
    soundlessly heel-and-toe
        practicing my Indian walk.

3

Past the abandoned quarry
    where the pale sun bobbed
        in the sump of the granite,
past copperhead ledge,
    where the ferns gave foothold,
        I walked, deliberate,

on to the clearing,
        with the stones in my pocket
                changing to oracles
and my coiled ear tuned
        to the slightest leaf-stir.
                I had kept my appointment.
There I stood in the shadow,
        at fifty measured paces,
                of the inexhaustible oak,
tyrant and target,
        Jehovah of acorns,
                watchtower of the thunders,
that locked King Philip's War
        in its annulated core
                under the cut of my name.
Father wherever you are
        I have only three throws
                bless my good right arm.
In the haze of afternoon,
        while the air flowed saffron,
                I played my game for keeps —
for love, for poetry,
        and for eternal life —
                after the trials of summer.

4

In the recurring dream
        my mother stands
                in her bridal gown
under the burning lilac,
        with Bernard Shaw and Bertie
                Russell kissing her hands;

the house behind her is in ruins;
 she is wearing an owl's face
  and makes barking noises.
Her minatory finger points.
 I pass through the cardboard doorway
  askew in the field
and peer down a well
 where an albino walrus huffs.
  He has the gentlest eyes.
If the dirt keeps sifting in,
 staining the water yellow,
  why should I be blamed?
Never try to explain.
 That single Model A
  sputtering up the grade
unfurled a highway behind
 where the tanks maneuver,
  revolving their turrets.
In a murderous time
 the heart breaks and breaks
  and lives by breaking.
It is necessary to go
 through dark and deeper dark
  and not to turn.
I am looking for the trail.
 Where is my testing-tree?
  Give me back my stones!

THE GAME

Let's spin the bottle
No I don't want to be kissed

Sometimes I feel my arm
Is turning into a tree

Or hardening to stone
Past memory of green

I've a long way to go
Who never learned to pray

O the night is coming on
And I am nobody's son

Father it's true
But only for a day

Notes

Around Pastor Bonhoeffer (page 12). Dietrich Bonhoeffer
was a German Lutheran pastor and theologian whose Chris-
tian conscience forced him, against the pacific temper of his
spirit, to accept the necessity of political activism and to join
in a conspiracy for the murder of Hitler. The plot failed, and
he was arrested by the Gestapo (1943). On April 9, 1945, he
was hanged at Flossenburg extermination camp. His brother
Klaus and two brothers-in-law were also destroyed. Some of
the details of the poem have their source in Bonhoeffer's two
posthumous publications, *The Cost of Discipleship* and *Letters
and Papers from Prison,* and in the biography by his disciple
Eberhard Bethge.

King of the River (page 15). Within two weeks after leav-
ing the ocean to swim up the rivers of the Northwest and
spawn, the bounding Pacific salmon degenerates into "an aged,
colorless, and almost lifeless fish." The same geriatric process
in humans takes some twenty to forty years.

Summer Solstice (page 25). I am indebted to Andrew Field
for helping me construe the Russian of this early lyric by
Mandelstam.

Tristia (page 26). Mandelstam's Latin title, meaning Poems
of Sorrow, alludes to the elegiac epistles of Ovid, which the
Roman poet began on his journey into exile in Tomis. Ovid
spoke of the sorrow of exile, of his unconquerable will to sur-
vive and to write, of his loves, and of his hope that he might
be allowed to return to Rome. Mandelstam never returned
from the prison camp to which Stalin sent him.

Hand-rolled Cigarettes (page 38). Devotees of the hand-rolled cigarette in Russia are said to be divided into opposite camps, according to their preference for rolling their tobacco in *Pravda* or *Izvestia,* the two top official newspapers. One of the jokes heard in Moscow literary circles has to do with a man who is sent to jail for a political crime. As soon as he is put behind bars, he is surrounded by prisoners who are eager for information about the outside world. "What's the news?" they inquire. "How should I know?" he replies, with a shrug. "I don't smoke."

Yevtushenko's poem is full of political allusions, beginning, in the second stanza, with Stalin's infamous fantasy of a Doctors' Plot. The last line of the poem parodies a celebrated boast by Khrushchev.

This is one of ten poems I have translated, with assistance from Anthony Kahn, for Yevtushenko's forthcoming *Stolen Apples* (Doubleday), a selection of his work made by the poet himself.

The Gladiators (page 42). The impulsive monk who tried to stop the bloodshed suffered his martyrdom at the hands of the enraged spectators about A.D. 400. The scandal of his dismemberment led to the proscription of man-to-man combats.

Bolsheviks (page 44). Aba Stolzenberg (1905–41) was an obscure Yiddish poet who came to the United States from Poland. Irving Howe, in the course of compiling *A Treasury of Yiddish Poetry* (Holt, Rinehart & Winston) in collaboration with Eliezer Greenberg, introduced me to Stolzenberg's work and assisted me with the text.

The Mound Builders (page 45). The civilization of the Mound Builders, of whom regrettably little is known, flourished between A.D. 900 and 1100. The site of their community in Georgia was later held sacred by the Creek Nation. At the time of my visit to the Ocmulgee National Monument, in the spring of 1962, President Kennedy had just announced the resumption of nuclear testing by the United States.

Boris Pasternak; Dante; Cleopatra (pages 51–54). Anna Akhmatova (1888–1966), friend and peer of Pasternak, is one of the great figures of modern Russian poetry. Max Hayward and I have worked in close collaboration for several years on a translation of her selected poems, of which these three are representative, to be published by Atlantic–Little, Brown.

The Bottom of the Glass (page 56). This poem is modeled on some untitled lines by the contemporary Russian poet Naum Korzhavin, a number of whose poems I have translated for *Pages from Tarusa: New Voices in Russian Writing* (Little, Brown), edited by Andrew Field.

The Testing-Tree (page 60). When I was a boy in Worcester, Massachusetts, my family lived on top of a hill, at the thin edge of the city, with the woods beyond. Much of the time I was alone, but I learned how not to be lonely, exploring the surrounding fields and the old Indian trails. In the games that I improvised, most of them involved with running, climbing, and a variety of ball-skills, I was a fierce competitor, representing in turn myself and my imaginary opponent. It did not occur to me to be surprised that "I" was always the winner.

The stone-throwing that figures in the poem was of a somewhat special order, since it did more than try my skill: it challenged destiny. My life hinged on the three throws permitted me, according to my rules. If I hit the target-oak once, somebody would love me; if I hit it twice, I should be a poet; if I scored all three times, I should never die. A friend of mine tells me that what I have recorded here is recognizable as an ancient ritual, and that the patriarchal scarred oak, as I have described it, is transparently a manifestation of the King of the Wood. Such mysteries for a Worcester childhood!